CW00536123

BRANCH LINES
AROUND
MARKET DRAYTON

From Wellington, Nantwich and Stoke-on-Trent

Vic Mitchell and Keith Smith

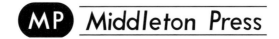

MP Middleton Press

Front cover: *Market Drayton was recorded as colour photography was becoming popular, but steam transport less so. The old goods shed is red, while the modern agricultural store is white. (Colour-Rail.com)*

Back cover: *The Railway Clearing House map for 1917 helps to explain the complexities of the area. The route on the left is featured in our* **Shrewsbury to Crewe** *album.*

Published October 2014

ISBN 978 1 908174 67 3

© Middleton Press, 2014

Design Deborah Esher
Typesetting Barbara Mitchell

Published by
    Middleton Press
    Easebourne Lane
    Midhurst
    West Sussex
    GU29 9AZ
Tel: 01730 813169
Fax: 01730 812601
Email: info@middletonpress.co.uk
www.middletonpress.co.uk

Printed in the United Kingdom by Henry Ling Limited, at the Dorset Press, Dorchester, DT1 1HD

CONTENTS

ACKNOWLEDGEMENTS

We are very grateful for the assistance received from many of those mentioned in the credits, also to A.R.Carder, A.J.Castledine, G.Croughton, R.Darvill, G.Gartside, S.C.Jenkins, D.K.Jones, N.Langridge, B.Lewis, J.P.McCrickard, A.Neale, Dr I.Picton-Robinson, Mr D. and Dr S.Salter, R.Yate and in particular our always supportive wives, Barbara Mitchell and Janet Smith.

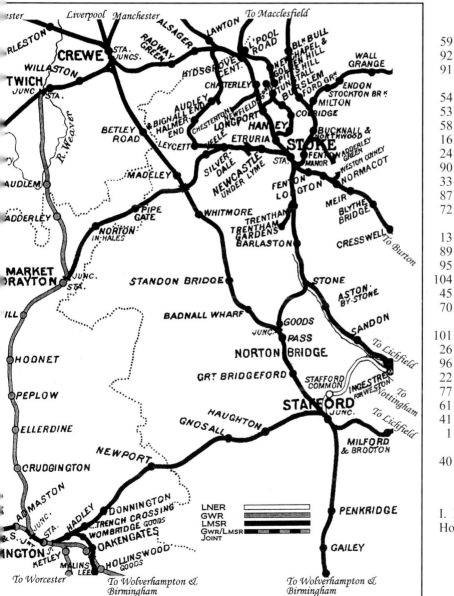

INDEX

I. Railway Clearing House map for 1947.

GEOGRAPHICAL SETTING

Stoke-on-Trent is situated at the southern extremity of the Pennines, where the ground forms a lower ridge. It is the location of the sources of the south flowing River Trent and also some Mersey tributaries, which mostly flow northwestwards. A gap in the ridge was chosen for the Stafford to Crewe main line, near to Madeley; the "Cheshire Gap".

Extensive coal and clay deposits around Stoke gave rise to much industry and the district becoming known as "The Potteries". The coal extended west to Newcastle and Madeley. The remainder of the route traversed mainly red sandstones, much of which has proved ideal for building purposes. The minerals have been little worked in recent times.

The majority of our journey ran over productive agricultural ground, drained at its southern end by northern tributaries of the River Severn. Some coal was also worked in the Wellington district.

Most of the track was in Shropshire, but the northern extremity was in Staffordshire and the Nantwich end was in Cheshire.

The maps are to the scale of 25ins to 1 mile, with north at the top, unless otherwise indicated.

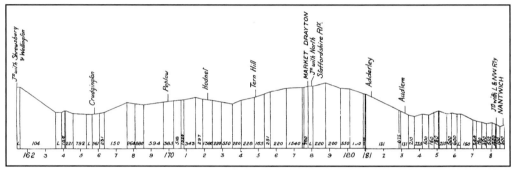

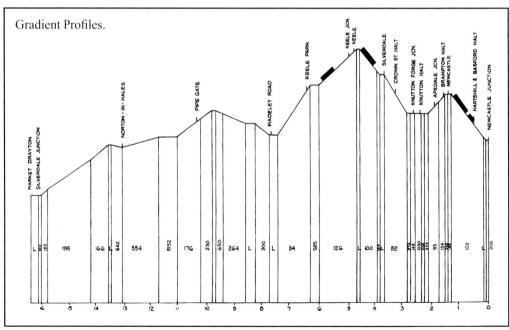

Gradient Profiles.

HISTORICAL BACKGROUND

The North Staffordshire Railway opened to Stoke-on-Trent from the south at Colwich in 1848. It continued north to Congleton that year, and also opened its line from Uttoxeter. A short branch west to Newcastle was opened on 6th September 1852, by the NSR. Here it met the Silverdale & Newcastle-under-Lyme Railway, which had opened between those places for freight in 1850. Passengers were carried from 7th April 1862, the route having been acquired by the NSR in 1859. The Nantwich & Market Drayton Railway opened its line between those places on 20th October 1863. It was taken over by the Great Western Railway in 1897. The GWR had opened north from Wellington to Market Drayton on 16th October 1867. Its trains had passed through Wellington since 1849, running between Wolverhampton and Shrewsbury. The NSR later extended further south, the route opening between Silverdale and Market Drayton on 1st February 1870. It also created the Audley Branch in 1870, but passenger service did not begin until 28th June 1880. It ended early, on 27th April 1931, but freight continued until 1963.

In 1923, the NSR became part of the London Midland & Scottish Railway. In 1948, this became the London Midland Region of British Railways, while the GWR formed its Western Region. Passenger service was withdrawn between Silverdale and Market Drayton on 7th May 1956 and from Nantwich to Wellington on 9th September 1963. Through freight trains ran on this route until 8th May 1967. The Stoke-on-Trent to Silverdale section lasted until 2nd March 1964. Freight traffic continued a little longer, details being given in the captions. The exception was that coal traffic lasted until 1998 from a colliery west of Newcastle to the Stafford-Crewe main line. Details follow.

PASSENGER SERVICES

Down trains running on at least five days per week are listed in the tables here: Prior to 1939, through coaches, from Manchester (London Road) were operated to Portsmouth and Bournemouth via our route. Details of the working were: attached to the 10.10 from Manchester to Euston, taken off at Crewe, and run to Wellington calling only at Market Drayton; then, departing with the Birkenhead to Bournemouth train, the through Portsmouth Harbour portion was detached at Eastleigh.

Wellington to Crewe

	Fast		Most Stations	
	Weekdays	Sundays	Weekdays	Sundays
1871	3	0	3	2
1901	0	0	6	1
1930	1	0	6	3
1951	0	0	6	2
1963	0	0	6	0

Stoke to Market Drayton

			Stoke to Newcastle only	
	Weekdays	Sundays	Weekdays	Sundays
1870	4	2	9	1
1890	4	2	9	2
1910	6	2	35	6
1931	5	2	5	0
1951	3	0	2	0
1963	-	-	2	0

The high 1910 figure was due to railcars operating between Stoke and Silverdale. They ran until 1923.

Audley Branch

	All Stations		To Leycett only	
	Weekdays	Sundays	Weekdays	Sundays
1919	7	2	3	0
1930	3	0	2	0

There was one extra train to Hammerhead for many years.

WELLINGTON, MARKET DRAYTON, NANTWICH, CREWE, and MANCHESTER.—Great Western.

Fares from Wellington. 1 cl. 2 cl. gov	Paddington Station,	mrn	mrn	mrn	aft	aft	aft		mrn	London Road Sta.,	mrn	mrn	mrn	aft	aft	aft		mrn	
	LONDON 36..dep.	1215	c	630	950	945		210	45	434 MANCHESTERdep.	835	1150	210	415	515	7 0			
0 9 0 6 0 4½	37 BIRMINGHAM* "	6 08	30	1040	1248	1 40		4 40	7 30	434 LEEDS (Nw) 431 "	6 0	9 25	1180	323	305	535			
1 6 1 0 0 9	50 WORCESTER †.. "		7 09	55	1035	1217		315	6 15	000 HUDDERSFLD 431 "		1046	1014	1223	94	100	3		
1 10 1 2 0 11	27 WELLINGTON "		7 59	20	01110	1 90		0 0	9 0	440 "									
2 9 1 9 1 4½	42 SHREWSBURY.. "	7 59	20	1040	1233	2 15		4 50	8 15	From Derby, see p.445.									

Right margin notes (Sundays, stops, etc.)

January 1901

STOKE-ON-TRENT, NEWCASTLE, HARDCASTLE, and MARKET DRAYTON.

Miles	Down.		mrn	mrn	mrn	mrn	mrn	aft S	aft	aft S	aft E	aft S
—	Stoke-on-Trent.........dep.		7 2	8 0	8 38	9 13	1220	1245	1255	2 45	3 10
2	Newcastle ¶	5 20	7 8	8 5	8 43	9 21	1225	1251	1 5	2 50	3 15
4½	Silverdale	5 30	7 18	8 12		9 28	1234	1257		2 57	3 22
6	Keele A	5 36	7 23	8 17		9 32	1238	1 1		3 1	3 26
7½	Leycett	5 41	7 30				1242			3 6	
9	Halmerend	5 47	7 37				1247			3 14	
10½	Audley and Bignall End		7 44				1252				
13¼	Alsager Road		7 53				1 0				
15¼	Harecastle B 626 to 633. arr.		8 0				1 10				
8½	Madeley Road		8 22		9 38		1 7				
11¾	Pipe Gate, for Woore		8 32		9 46		1 13				3 42
14	Norton-in-Hales		8 39		9 53		1 19				3 48
17¾	Market Drayton 61a...arr.		850		10 0		1 26				3 55
34	61a WELLINGTON ...... arr.				1047		2 13				6 20
44¼	61a SHREWSBURY (General).. "				1115		3 1				7 19

November 1930

November 1930

WELLINGTON, MARKET DRAYTON, NANTWICH, and CREWE.

Mls. from Wellington	Down.		mrn	mrn		mrn	Week Days.		mrn	mrn		aft	aft			Sundays.				mrn	aft
	108 London (Paddington)...dep.	1 30		6 30		1119		11 10		2 10	6 10			1210	1210	1010	1 10			
	108 BIRMINGHAM (Snow Hill)...	6 5	8 35		1035		2 23		4 15	8 15			6 45	7 0	1 30	3 28				
	116 WORCESTER (Sh. H.) 108 "		6 35		9 32		2 27		2 6	22					1050	1050				
	111 SHREWSBURY A 485... "	6 58	9 10		1125		2 35		2 53	5 10	8 12		7 45	8 52	2 10	5 5				
—	Wellington ....dep.	7 35	9 30		1146	3 16		3 40	5 50	9 27			8 15	9 15	3 20	5 40				
4½	Crudgington ❋	7 43	9 59		1154			3 48	6 09	35			8 22	9 23	3 28	5 50				
8½	Peplow ¶	7 52	10 8		12 2			3 57	6 9	9 44				9 32	3 39	6 0				
11	Hodnet	7 53	10 13		12 7			4 2	6 16	9 49				9 37	3 44	6 9				
13½	Tern Hill	8 5	10 19		1213			4 10	6 23	9 56				9 43	3 50	6 12				
16¾	Market Drayton 639 {arr.	8 13	10 28		1220			4 18	6 30	10 3				9 49	3 56	6 19				
	{dep.	8 18	10 30		1225			4 20	6 36	10 6			9 50	9 50		6 22				
20¼	Adderley	8 23	10 35		1232			4 25	6 44	‡						6 33				
22	Audlem	8 30	10 42		1237			4 30	6 54	1018			10 13			6 43				
27¾	Nantwich 486.....[520 542]	8 39	10 10		1247			4 38	7 8	1027			10 21			6 51				
32	Crewe 413, 422, 494, arr.	8 45	11 2		1256		3 58	4 49	7 20	1035			3 47			9 15				
62¾	520 MANCHESTER (Lon. Rd.) arr.	9 55	12 30		2 10		4 50	6 8	8 15	1 35										

Mls. from Crewe	Up.		mrn	mrn		mrn	Week Days.		non	aft		aft	aft	aft		Sundays.			mrn	mrn	aft
—	522 MANCHESTER (Lon..Rd.). dep.		8 35		1010		12 0		4 10	5 30	7 10			9 15						
—	Crewe ....dep.	6 25	9 35		11 0		1 0		5 5	6 35	8 10		6 45	11 0						
4½	Nantwich	6 35	9 43				1 10		5 13	6 43	8 19		6 53	11 8						
10	Audlem	6 45	9 55				1 20		5 24	6 54	8 32		7 3	1118						
11¾	Adderley	6 50	10 1				1 25		5 29	6 59	839									
15¼	Market Drayton 639 {arr.	6 57	10 8		1119		1 32		5 36	7 7	8 48		7 14	1132	4 25					
	{dep.	7 2	1011		1120		1 36		5 40	7 12		8 50	7 23	1135	4 31					
18¼	Tern Hill	7 8	1017				1 42		5 46	7 18		9 0	7 29	1140	4 31					
21	Hodnet.	7 14	1023				1 47		5 52	7 24		9 7	7 39	1147	4 36					
23½	Peplow ¶	7 19	1028				1 52		5 55	7 29		9 15	7 48	1152	4 41					
27½	Crudgington	7 32	1033				2 3		6 0	7 40		9 25	7 57	1211	4 55					
32	Wellington 108, 111, 485 arr.	7 42	1047		1143		2 13		6 20	7 50				5 5						
42¼	108 SHREWSBURY A 485... arr.	8 47	1115		1255		3 1	7 19	9 8			9 54	8 55	1	1 45	9 36				
58	111 WORCESTER (Sh.H.) 118 "	10 56	1 50		2 53		4 55	9 26					12 49		2 18	6 25				
64	111 BIRMINGHAM (Snow Hill) "	8 55	1156		1240		3 43	7 39			1015	1138	10 30	1 2	2 18	6 25				
174¼	111 London (Paddington)... "	11 02	0		4 20		4 30	10 8			4 10		1 40		6 20	9 0				

A General. A Saturday night. B Departs Manchester (London Rd.) at 5 5 Saturdays. ‡ Foregate Street. ‡ Stops at 10 12 aft. on Sats. ¶ "Halt" at Ellerdine, between Crudgington and Peplow. S or Ş Sats only.

March 1951

Table 133 STOKE-ON-TRENT, NEWCASTLE, and MARKET DRAYTON

Miles		a.m	a.m E	a.m W	p.m S	p.m	p.m U		
—	Stoke-on-Trent.....dep.	7 34	8 36	9 5	1242	5 0	6 40	..	..
1¾	Newcastle	7 43	8 41	9 11	1247	5 5	6 46	..	..
2¾	Liverpool Road Halt.				1249	5 7			
4½	Silverdale	7 50		9 18	1253	5 11	6 53		
5¾	Keele A	7 53		9 22	1256	5 14			
11	Pipe Gate, for Woore	8 8		9 33	1 6	5 25			
13¼	Norton-in-Hales	8 15		9 39	1 12	5 30			
16¼	Market Drayton ....arr.	8 22		9 46	1 19	5 37			

Miles		a.m Z	a.m Y	a.m E	a.m W	a.m	p.m S	p.m LR	p.m V	p.m
—	Market Drayton.....dep.	..	..	..	8 42	1218	1 45	..	7 0	..
3¼	Norton-in-Hales	..	..	..	8 48	1224	1 51	..	7 7	..
5¼	Pipe Gate, for Woore	..	..	..	8 54	1230	1 57	..	7 15	..
11¾	Keele A	..	..	..	9 6	1242	2 9	..	7 24	..
12½	Silverdale	7 9	7 44	..	9 9	1245	2 13	..	7 29	..
14¾	Liverpool Road Halt.	7 16	7 48	..			2 18	..		..
15	Newcastle	7 21	7 52	8 50	9 15	1254	2 21	4 17	7 39	..
16¾	Stoke-on-Trent.....arr	7 28	7 58	8 57	9 22	1 1	2 27	4 22	7 47	..

A Station for Little Madeley & Madeley Heath (1 mile)
E Except Saturdays
R Through Carriages to Birmingham arr. 6 30 p.m (Table 124)
S Saturdays only
U Through Carriages from Birmingham dep. 4 50 p.m. (Table 124)
V Through Carriages to Staffordarc 8 28 p.m. (Table 124)
Y Through Carriages to Birmingham arr. 10 16 a.m. (Table 124)
Z Through Carriages to Birmingham arr. 9 16 a.m. (Table 124)
W Train temporarily withdrawn

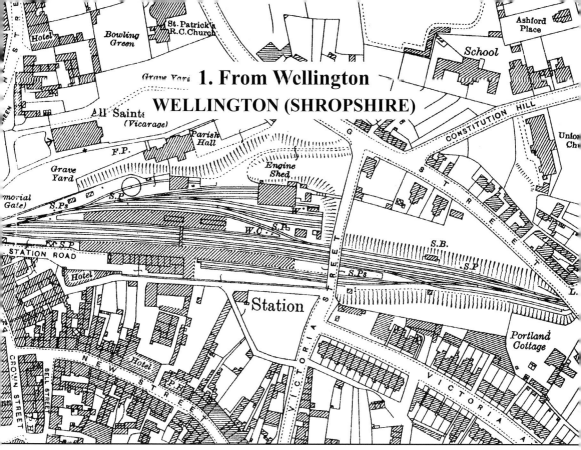

1. From Wellington
WELLINGTON (SHROPSHIRE)

II.　　This map is from 1927. The name carried the suffix "(Salop)" in the early BR years and "for Telford" from 16th May 1983. This was changed to "Telford West" on 12th May 1986, to reduce confusion, and dropped on 28th May 1994. Shropshire was added from 29th September 1996.

1.　　The station was unusual in that it opened with four through tracks. The two platforms were then fairly short and the engine shed, shown on the map, was originally the goods shed. LMS "Prince of Wales" class 3P 4-6-0 no. 25845 waits with a Stafford to Shrewsbury local train on 3rd August 1935. (H.F.Wheeler/R.S.Carpenter coll.)

2.   The two bay platforms are on the left of this westward view from 1956. Staff serving passenger traffic numbered 45 in 1923 and 38 in 1933. All were GWR employees. Its goods yard had 30 in 1923; it was merged with the LMS in 1933. The GWR goods staff numbered 36 at that time. (Stations UK)

3.   A view west from platform 3 in the 1950s features the bridge at the north end of Market Square and No. 3 signal box, of 1913. It had 58 levers and closed on 30th September 1973. Most of the buildings were completed in around 1880. (Lens of Sutton coll.)

4.   Ex-GWR class 2301 0-6-0 no. 2516 takes water on 23rd April 1955, while working "The Shropshire Rail Tour". Station Road is behind the wall and it terminates at the main building, the roof light of which is evident above the tender. The engine retired to the Museum of the GWR in Swindon. (Unknown)

5.　　Seen in May 1959 at platform 6 is ex-GWR 5101 class 2-6-2T no. 4158 waiting to run south to Much Wenlock. This bay platform was taken out of use on 8th March 1969. The adjacent one was used for local trains to Walsall for many years subsequently. (Unknown)

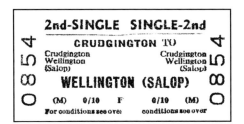

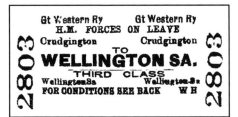

6.   The shed was photographed on 8th September 1962 with 0-6-0PTs nos 9774 and 3792 nearest. On the left is class 2 2-6-2T no. 41201 of 1946. The end for the depot came on 10th August 1964. (L.W.Rowe)

7.   Ex-GWR 0-6-0PT no. 9636 was involved with relaying on 7th April 1963. On the left is No. 2 Box, which had a 71-lever frame in use from 15th March 1953 until 13th May 2002. Near to it is no. D1000 *Western Enterprise*, the first of its class and completed in 1961. (Unknown)

8.   Nos 150149 and 150146 were recorded working the 13.28 Birmingham New Street to Aberystwyth on 24th June 1989. The line to the remaining bay platform is in the foreground. It had earlier been used by Coalport trains. (T.Heavyside)

Other views of the station can be found in our
Craven Arms to Wellington, Stafford to Wellington
and *Wolverhampton to Shrewsbury* **albums.**

9.   The second barrow crossing is evident in this view from 25th August 1993. The spacious No. 2 Box took over the working of Stafford Junction, 1¼ miles to the east, upon the demise of the box there on 10th September 1967. The work of No. 2 was taken over by Madeley Junction until 19th November 2012, since when the area has been controlled by the West Midlands Signalling Centre, at Saltley. (M.A.Turvey)

10.   A glimpse of the up platform on 26th June 2008 shows railings on the site of the former Platform 1 and a car park on the area occupied by the engine shed and depot. At least, all the buildings on both sides were intact. (V.Mitchell)

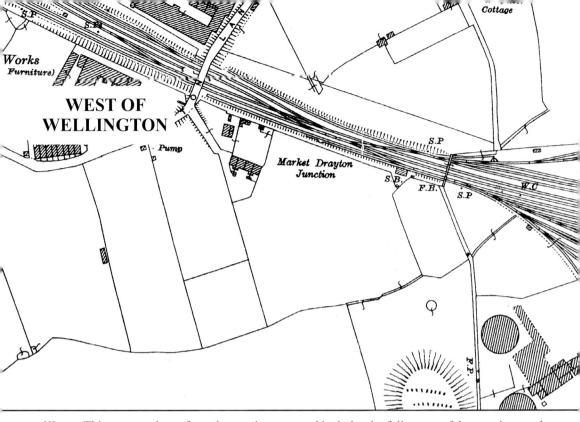

Works
(Furniture)

WEST OF
WELLINGTON

Pump

Market Drayton
Junction

S.B.   F.B.   S.P   W.C

Cottage

S.P

F.P.

III.   This map continues from the previous one and includes the full extent of the massive goods yard which served this important commercial and manufacturing centre. Top left is the 1867 route diverging to Market Drayton. The circle on the left hand page indicates a gas holder. The works had its own siding from 1870 until 1968 and the timber yard had two from prior to 1870 and another from that year, until all were lost in 1962.

11.   A panorama from Bridge Road on 9th August 1932 has the former LNWR goods yard on the right of the two running lines and the GWR goods yard on the left. Nearest are its cattle pens. Its siding is concreted to aid dung removal. The crane on the left was rated at 10 tons.
(Mowat coll./Brunel University.)

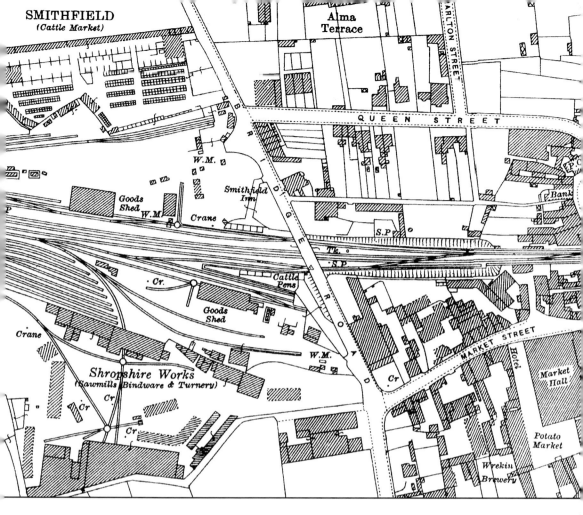

12. Seen from the footbridge on the same day is Market Drayton Junction. The lines to that town curve under the right arch. No. 4 Box of 1881 had 46 levers and closed on 30th September 1973. (Mowat coll./Brunel University)

LONGDON HALT

13.   A northward view in 1950 has a tanker running on the B5063, towards the village. Tended gardens were unusual at a halt. This one opened on 20th October 1934. (Stations UK)

14.   The Clee Hills are in the distance in this record from 29th August 1960. The guard would deliver and remove lamps as necessary. Closure came on 9th June 1963.
(W.A.Camwell/SLS coll.)

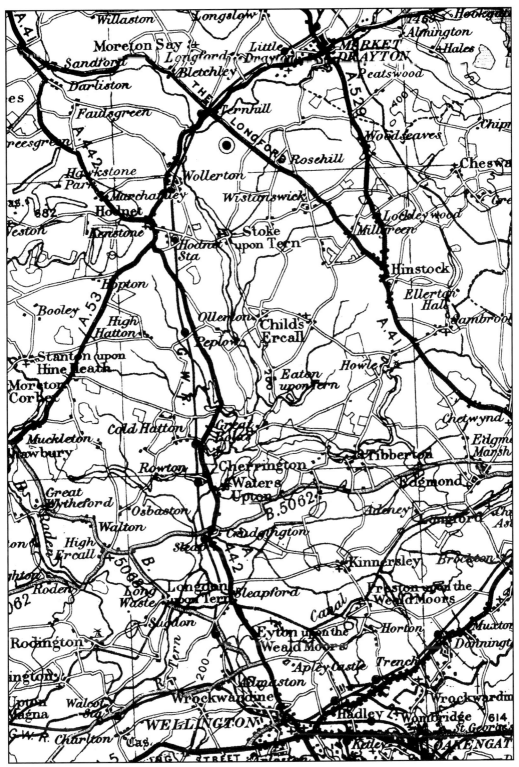

IV.   The 1946 edition is reproduced at 1 ins to 2 miles to show the location of all stops to Market Drayton. There were several airfields in the area during World War II, but only one is shown and only one remains. A black dot within a circle is used for it. All halts, except Little Drayton, are illustrated sequentially.

15.   The halt is seen not long before closure, devoid of flowers and with rotting nameboards. The hills are hidden in mist. The initial cost had been around £290. No. 9774 was an 0-6-0PT, which entered service in March 1936. (P.Ward/SLS coll.)

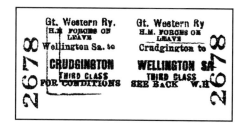

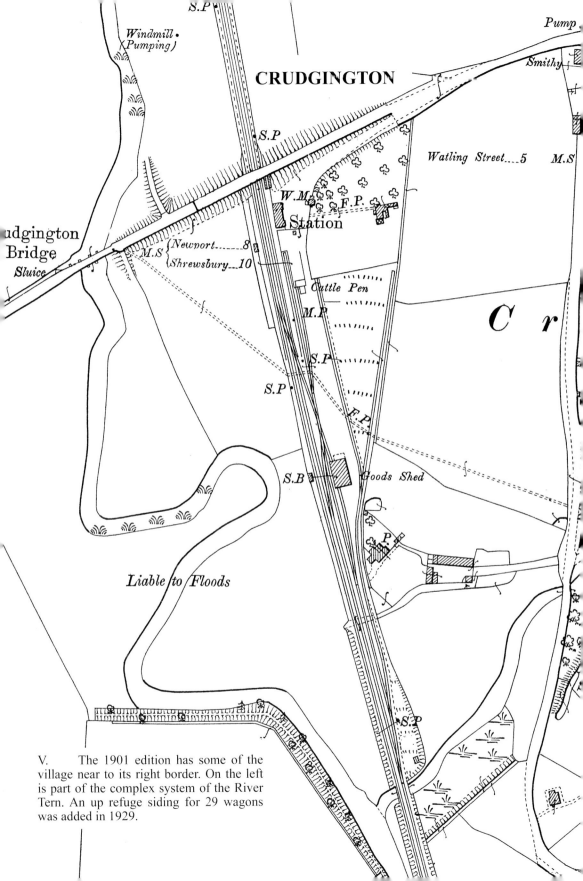

Windmill
(Pumping)

S.P

Pump

Smithy

CRUDGINGTON

S.P

Watling Street....5   M.S

W.M. F.P.
Station

udgington
Bridge

M.S {Newport....8
Shrewsbury....10

Sluice

Cattle Pen

M.P

C r

S.P

S.P

F.P

S.B Goods Shed

P.

Liable to Floods

S.P

V.   The 1901 edition has some of the
village near to its right border. On the left
is part of the complex system of the River
Tern. An up refuge siding for 29 wagons
was added in 1929.

16.   The map confirms that there were initially steps only to the up platform, passengers having to cross the tracks on the level to and from the other one. There was a staff of seven in 1903-31. (P.Laming coll.)

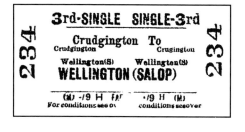

3rd-SINGLE   SINGLE-3rd
234   Crudgington   To
Crudgington   Crudgington
Wellington(S)   Wellington(S)
WELLINGTON (SALOP)   234
(M) -/9 H FAL   -/9 H (M)
For conditions see on   conditions see over

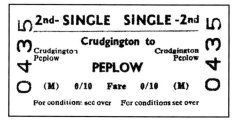

2nd- SINGLE   SINGLE -2nd
0435   Crudgington to
Crudgington   Crudgington
Peplow   Peplow
PEPLOW   0435
(M)   0/10   Fare   0/10   (M)
For conditions see over   For conditions see over

17.   A similar view in 1950 reveals the later steps and that ivy has gone out of fashion. No. 7207 is a 2-8-2T of the GWR's 7200 class and is passing over the barrow crossing. The ornate brickwork was red and cream. (Stations U K)

18.   Most of the frontage is now visible, the date being 10th April 1957. It seems that the newspapers have just arrived. The goods shed contained a 30cwt crane. (H.C.Casserley)

19.　　"Mixed Freight" was a term justifiably often used. Sadly no details were recorded, but this through traffic lasted until 8th May 1967, almost four years after passenger service had ceased. (P.Ward/SLS coll.)

20.   Not appearing in the other views is the end-loading dock, right. It seems that a parcels shed had been built on much of it, using asbestos sheets. A train approaches from the north on 30th June 1962. (R.M.Casserley)

21.   The remainder of the dock together with its cattle pens, can be seen in this view from 7th July 1963. Beyond them are the grain stores and on the right is the 1893 21-lever signal box, which closed on 6th March 1967. Goods traffic ceased here on 3rd May 1965. (P.J.Garland/R.S.Carpenter coll.)

ROWTON HALT

22.   A 1950 photograph shows the inconspicuous structure, which came into use on 29th June 1935. Nearby was the bridge carrying the road to the village of Stych Lane. The halt was busy during the war, serving both Army and RAF camps. (Stations UK)

23.   A southward view on 10th April 1957 includes the portable wooden steps provided for the less agile. The platforms were only suitable for two coaches and closed on 9th September 1963. (H.C.Casserley)

ELLERDINE HALT

24.   The halt opened on 7th July 1930 and is seen exactly 33 years later, along with its public goods siding. This was in use from 28th February 1928. (P.J.Garland/R.S.Carpenter coll.)

25.   Seen on the same day is the shed which covered the ground frame. There was a path from the road to the down platform (left) and steps to the up one. Their closure came on 9th September 1963. (P.J.Garland/R.S.Carpenter coll.)

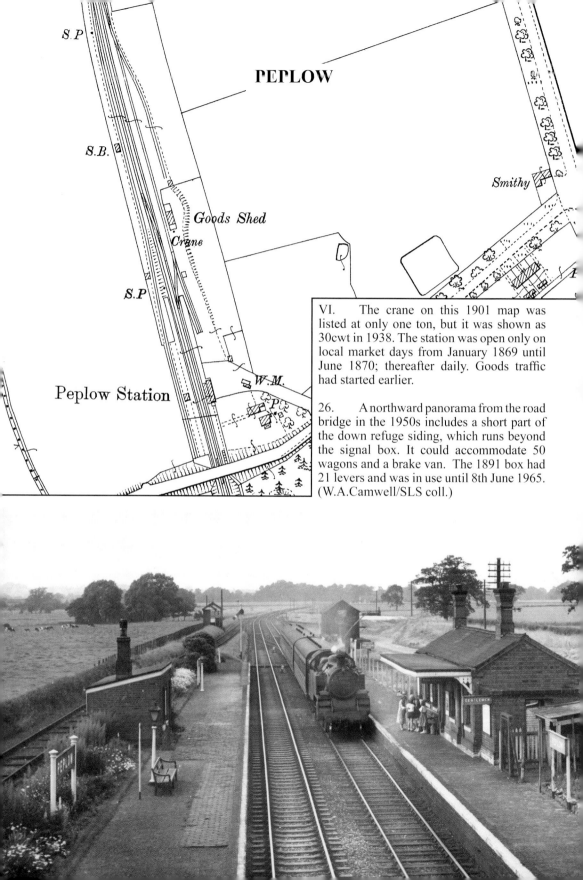

PEPLOW

S.P

S.B.

Goods Shed

Crane

S.P

Smithy

Peplow Station

W.M.

P

VI.   The crane on this 1901 map was listed at only one ton, but it was shown as 30cwt in 1938. The station was open only on local market days from January 1869 until June 1870; thereafter daily. Goods traffic had started earlier.

26.   A northward panorama from the road bridge in the 1950s includes a short part of the down refuge siding, which runs beyond the signal box. It could accommodate 50 wagons and a brake van. The 1891 box had 21 levers and was in use until 8th June 1965. (W.A.Camwell/SLS coll.)

27.   The siding was on a lesser gradient than the main line, which falls under the bridge at 1 in 385. It made the siding safer, being almost level. The date is 10th April 1957. (R.M.Casserley)

28.   Ex-GWR 0-6-0PT no. 9774 arrives with a single coach forming the 12.50pm Wellington to Market Drayton on 29th July 1961. There is evidence that the nearby shelter was provided with winter heating. (E.Wilmshurst)

29.	The interior is seen in May 1962 and it has many GWR features, notably the crowd control barrier. On the right is a side view of the parcel scales. RAF Peplow was served from 1941 to 1949. (R.G.Nelson/T.Walsh coll.)

30.	The case under the clock face housed a long pendulum, while the hearth served for chalked departure times. The walls were coated with distemper which soon flaked and the lampless bracket did little to improve the environs. (R.G.Nelson/T.Walsh coll.)

31.   On 29th July 1961, we see the 12.15pm Wellington to Crewe. The black hut was the lamp room and was made of iron for safety reasons. There were four employees here in 1923-46. (E.Wilmshurst)

32.   Our last visit is on 7th July 1963 and the busy goods yard was in use until 3rd May 1965. The canopy was cantilevered to avoid the need for supports. The main commodity loaded here was sugar beet. (P.J.Garland/R.S.Carpenter coll.)

HODNET

VII. The 1902 edition includes the cattle market and the workhouse, the latter being a refuge for the destitute. Refuge for up and down trains, however, was provided by the 1928 extension of the center track as a siding, seen at the bottom.

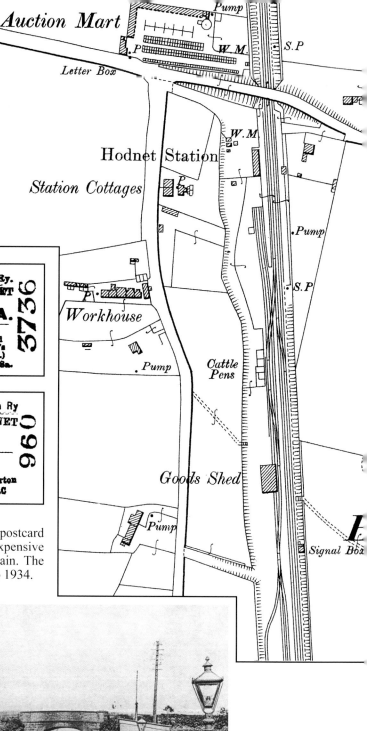

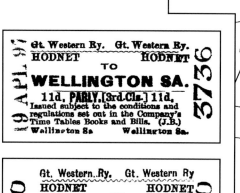

33. All was tidy for the postcard photographer, in about 1910. Expensive architecture was justified here again. The men numbered eight from 1903 to 1934. (P.Laming coll.)

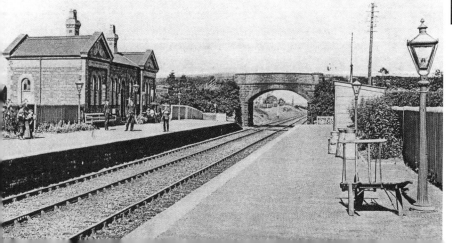

34.   There is evidence of another important rural traffic - milk. Churns were used until the mid-1930s, very widely. This postcard was franked in 1908. (P.Laming coll.)

35.   The box had a 17-lever frame and was in use until 6th March 1967. The letters were hung on the wall to signify messages to the engineering staff looking out from passing trains. (R.S.Carpenter coll.)

36.   A northward view in 1962 includes a train from Crewe and the sole member of staff. He obviously was an experienced gardener. (Stations UK)

37.   The hanging signs had long gone with improved telephonic communication. The pole carries extra connections in this 1962 picture of 0-6-0PT no. 9639 shunting. (Stations UK)

38.   Two views from 7th July 1963 complete our survey. This includes the 6-ton crane and the cattle pens on the dock. The timber trade needed to load heavy trunks. (P.J.Garland/R.S.Carpenter coll.)

39.   Passengers had to suffer no weather protection and a long walk along the road to the up platform, after buying their tickets, also no heating once there. At least, they could enjoy the polychromatic brickwork. (P.J.Garland/R.S.Carpenter coll.)

WOLLERTON HALT

40.   A southward view from July 1963 shows the platform suitable for 2½ coaches, which opened on 2nd November 1931 and closed on 9th September 1963. The shelters were of corrugated iron and the site was close to the village. (P.J.Garland/R.S.Carpenter coll.)

3rd-SINGLE   SINGLE-3rd
Wollerton Halt to
Wollerton Halt   Wollerton Halt
Hodnet   Hodnet
HODNET
(M),   0/4   FARE   0/4   (M)
For conditions see over   For conditions see over

1061

3rd · SINGLE   SINGLE · 3rd
ELLERDINE HALT TO
Ellerdine Halt   Ellerdine Halt
Market Drayton   Market Drayton
MARKET DRAYTON
(M)   1/6   Fare   1/6   (M)
For conditions see over   For conditions see over

1133

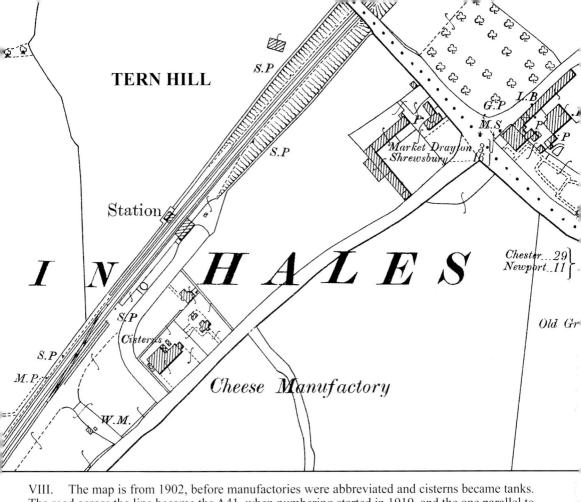

TERN HILL

S.P

S.P

Station

I N *H A L E S*

S.P
Cisterns
S.P
M.P.
W.M.

Cheese Manufactory

Market Drayton 3
Shrewsbury 16

G.P
M.S
I.B
P

Chester 29
Newport 11

Old Gr

VIII.   The map is from 1902, before manufactories were abbreviated and cisterns became tanks. The road across the line became the A41, when numbering started in 1919, and the one parallel to it was to be the A53.

41.   The structures were of a later GWR style, as the station did not open until 3rd April 1899. However, the goods yard opened with the line. It was expanded in 1915. (P.Laming coll.)

42. The footbridge was added in 1942, as traffic increased with two RAF and one Naval airfield being created nearby. In the distance is the 1894 17-lever signal box, which was in use until 30th October 1964 and is seen in 1957. The black shelter had come from Little Drayton Halt in 1943. (H.C.Casserley)

43.   A Crewe train calls on 29th July 1961, as one passenger speeds up the steps to catch it. The timber extension was probably for parcel traffic. (E.Wilmshurst)

44.   The contrasting bricks were red and yellow and the facilities for gentlemen had top ventilation. The photograph is from July 1963. Closure came on 9th September of that year, but the goods yard was in use until 10th August 1964. (P.J.Garland/R.S.Carpenter coll.)

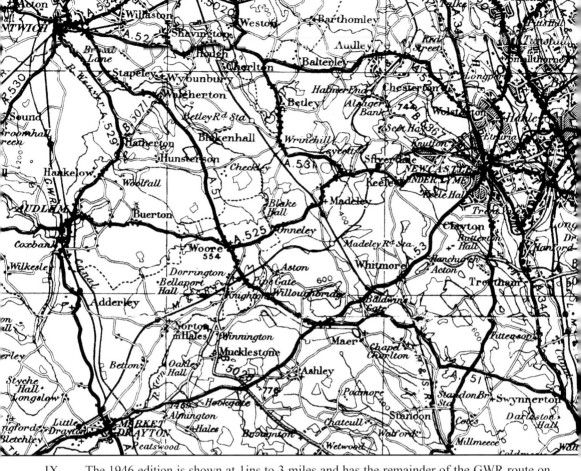

IX.   The 1946 edition is shown at 1ins to 3 miles and has the remainder of the GWR route on the left. The closed stations are shown with clear circles.

X.   An enlargement of the Market Drayton area at 1ins to 2 miles shows one station, one halt and two canal wharves. Little Drayton Halt was only open from 14th September 1935 until 6th October 1941 and seems to have been neglected by photographers.

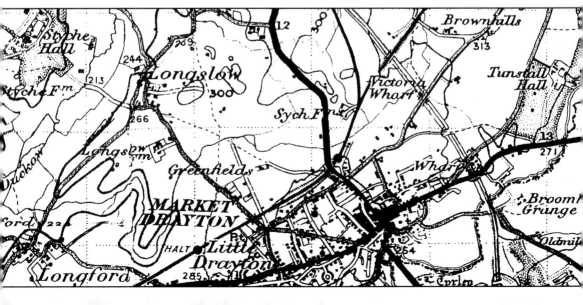

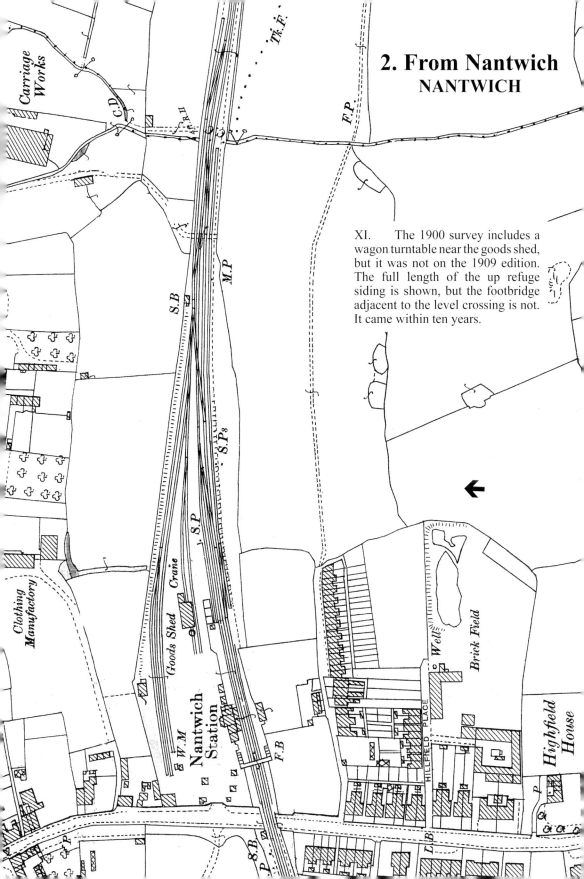

2. From Nantwich
NANTWICH

Carriage Works

C.D.

Tk.F.

F.P.

F.P.

XI.   The 1900 survey includes a wagon turntable near the goods shed, but it was not on the 1909 edition. The full length of the up refuge siding is shown, but the footbridge adjacent to the level crossing is not. It came within ten years.

S.B

M.P

S.P8

S.P

Clothing Manufactory

Goods Shed

Crane

Nantwich Station

W.M

F.B

Well

Brick Field

HILLFIELD PLACE

Highfield House

S.B

L.B

45.   The station was known as "Nantwich Junction" in 1864-1916 and was LNWR property, the company having opened it on 1st September 1858 for its Shrewsbury to Crewe service. (P.Laming coll.)

46.   A September 1952 record from the second footbridge includes "Station" on the box nameboard, although Nantwich Goods Yard Box had closed on 3rd December 1949. The box was fitted with a 30-lever frame and was still in use in 2014. (Bentley coll.)

47.   A 1956 record includes the once-popular "Hawkseye" nameboard of the LMSR and the redundant Goods Yard Box, in the distance. This also appears on the map. (H.F.Wheeller/R.S.Carpenter coll.)

48.   Both footbridges can be found in this panorama from 5th August 1963, when gas lighting was still in favour. The canopy and the main building had been extended southwards, due to increased parcel traffic. Cotton, shoes and gloves were their common contents.(R.M.Casserley)

49.	It is 1st June 1981 and no. 47488 is heading for Crewe. Cheese and salt had been important products at Nantwich until the coming of the railway. (T.Heavyside)

50.	Other uses were found for the main building, but the footbridge and canopies were removed, the goods yard having been closed on 4th September 1972. There had been a 5-ton crane. (Colour-Rail.com)

For other views of this station, see our *Shrewsbury to Crewe* album, pictures 70 to 79.

51.   No. M50668 is working the 14.00 Aberystwyth to Crewe service on 1st June 1981. The box had been in use at Wem North in 1942-48. Full lifting barriers arrived later and the platform for window cleaning was removed. (T.Heavyside)

SOUTH OF NANTWICH

52.   About ½ mile from the station, we come to Market Drayton Junction, a name used again just west of Wellington. The 22-lever 1884 signal box is seen about five years before being put out of action by a fire on 16th January 1967. (Milepost 92½)

COOLE PILATE HALT

53.   The halt was opened on 17th August 1935 and was in use until 9th September 1963. It was entirely of timber construction, as was the pedestrian crossing. A decoy town was created nearby in 1942 to give the impression to Nazi bombers that it was Crewe. Portsmouth was also simulated near the branch line to Hayling, but it was also kept secret. A later Defence Radar Station was developed during the Cold War as a potential seat of government. The lane at Hack Green was thus upgraded and provided with a flat-roofed 20-lever signal box. It was in use from 23rd July 1957 until 6th March 1967, in place of manned gates. (F.W.Shuttleworth)

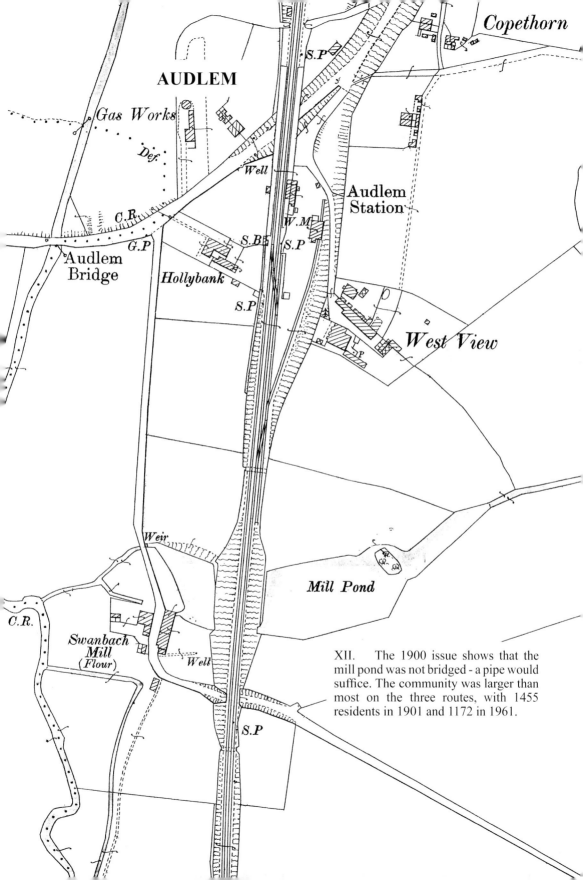

Copethorn

AUDLEM

Gas Works

Def.

C.R.

G.P

Audlem
Bridge

Hollybank

Well

Audlem
Station

S.P

S.B

W.M

S.P

S.P

West View

Weir

Mill Pond

C.R.

Swanbach
Mill
(Flour)

Well

S.P

XII.   The 1900 issue shows that the
mill pond was not bridged - a pipe would
suffice. The community was larger than
most on the three routes, with 1455
residents in 1901 and 1172 in 1961.

54.   This southward view in poor weather is from 10th April 1957. The 1889 signal box was closed on 23rd June 1957 and the box at Hack Green took over as a block post. The signals vanished and a ground frame was provided for access to the yard. (H.C.Casserley)

55.   It is about 1960 and a train bound for Crewe obstructs the foot crossing. Of note is the fact that the tiny down waiting room was heated. On the right is the end of the dock. The locomotive is class 3 2-6-2T no. 82009. (W.A.Camwell/SLS coll.)

56.   Seen on 9th July 1961, the shed on the left would contain the recording equipment for the weighbridge, which is in the foreground. Many cars from the mid-1930s were still in use, as none were produced during the war years. (Bentley coll.)

57.   The 5.18pm Crewe to Wellington was recorded on 26th April 1962. The station was open from 20th October 1863 until 9th September 1963, but goods traffic continued until 3rd February 1964. There had been a staff of ten in 1903, dropping to five by 1933. (R.G.Nelson/T.Walsh coll.)

COXBANK HALT

58.   The halt was only ¾ mile from Audlem and was open from 2nd June 1934 until 9th September 1963. Looking south, we can see both sets of steps on 10th April 1957. (R.M.Casserley)

2nd · SINGLE   SINGLE · 2nd
1675   1675
Market Drayton to
Market Drayton   Market Drayton
Cox Bank   Cox Bank
COX BANK
(M)   1/3   Fare   1/3   (M)
For conditions see over   For conditions see over

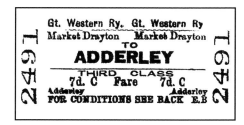

Gt. Western Ry. Gt. Western Ry
Market Drayton   Market Drayton
2491   2491
TO
ADDERLEY
THIRD   CLASS
7d. C   Fare   7d. C
Adderley   Adderley
FOR CONDITIONS SEE BACK E.B

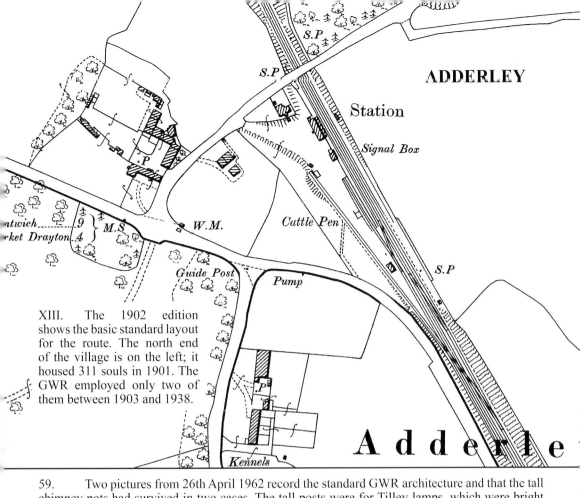

ADDERLEY

Station

Signal Box

S.P

S.P

Cattle Pen

S.P

W.M.

atwich
ket Drayton

9
4

M.S

Guide Post

Pump

P

Kennels

A d d e r l e

XIII. The 1902 edition shows the basic standard layout for the route. The north end of the village is on the left; it housed 311 souls in 1901. The GWR employed only two of them between 1903 and 1938.

59.   Two pictures from 26th April 1962 record the standard GWR architecture and that the tall chimney pots had survived in two cases. The tall posts were for Tilley lamps, which were bright due to the oil being pressurised. (R.G.Nelson/T.Walsh coll.)

60.　　The 1891 signal box housed 17 levers and was in use until 18th December 1963, when all service ceased here. Included is one of the smallest goods sheds on the route. (R.G.Nelson/T.Walsh coll.)

This is the final photograph of a Western Region station in our developing encyclopedia, the Southern having taken 18 years to complete. The Western took 21.

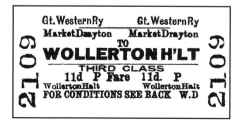

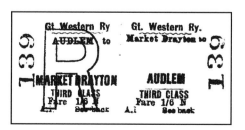

3. From Stoke-on-Trent

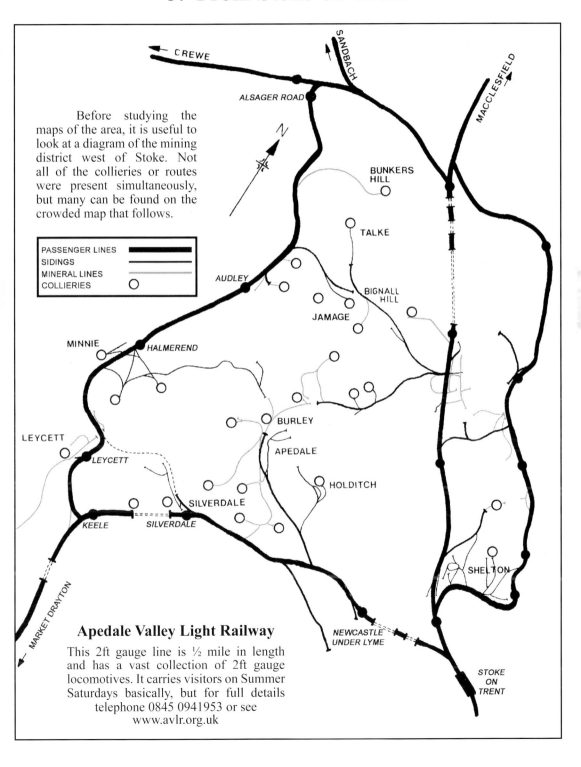

Before studying the maps of the area, it is useful to look at a diagram of the mining district west of Stoke. Not all of the collieries or routes were present simultaneously, but many can be found on the crowded map that follows.

CREWE

SANDBACH

MACCLESFIELD

ALSAGER ROAD

BUNKERS HILL

TALKE

PASSENGER LINES	▬▬▬
SIDINGS	—
MINERAL LINES	—
COLLIERIES	○

AUDLEY

BIGNALL HILL

JAMAGE

MINNIE

HALMEREND

LEYCETT

LEYCETT

BURLEY

APEDALE

HOLDITCH

KEELE

SILVERDALE

SILVERDALE

MARKET DRAYTON

SHELTON

Apedale Valley Light Railway

NEWCASTLE UNDER LYME

STOKE ON TRENT

This 2ft gauge line is ½ mile in length and has a vast collection of 2ft gauge locomotives. It carries visitors on Summer Saturdays basically, but for full details telephone 0845 0941953 or see www.avlr.org.uk

XIV. The 1947 edition at 1 ins to 1 mile is included to give an impression of the extent of the urban areas. Lower right, Stoke station is shown as rectangular, as is nearby Newcastle's. Our journey continues on the north side of Silverdale and through Silverdale Tunnel to Keele, now a university town. It runs south, through Keele Tunnel; the short Stoney Low Tunnel is just beyond the lower border. The Audley Branch curves along the left border, its stations being shown as white circles, due to their earlier closure.

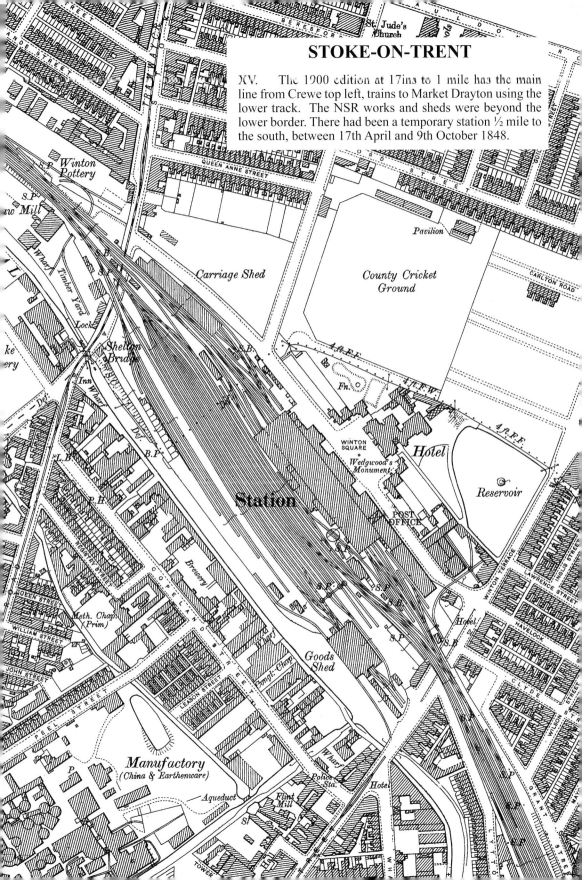

STOKE-ON-TRENT

XV.   The 1900 edition at 17ins to 1 mile has the main line from Crewe top left, trains to Market Drayton using the lower track. The NSR works and sheds were beyond the lower border. There had been a temporary station ½ mile to the south, between 17th April and 9th October 1848.

61.   The northeast elevation graced a postcard posted in 1908, while Wedgwood's statue faced the station. His potteries employed about 8000 by the 1980s and, together with Spode and Royal Doulton, made almost 80% of British ceramics. This included sanitary fittings. The district thus justified the term "The Potteries". (P.Laming coll.)

62.   The splendid building was completed in 1848. Gas and electric lighting are evident, the latter arriving in 1894, along with NSR's own generator. It was near the southern subway. (LOSA)

63.   This single span roof had replaced a three-span structure in 1894. It is seen from a train departing south in 1948. (Stations UK)

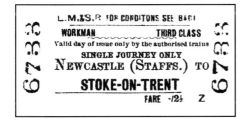

64.   Platform 1 and the main building are on the right in this 1957 view. The suffix "-on-Trent" came into use in 1923-24. (Stations UK)

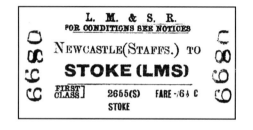

65.   A 1966 view in the same direction shows electrification work starting. No. 42727 is an ex-LMSR "Crab" class 2-6-0 and is on the one remaining through line. The other two became bidirectional. (Stations UK)

66.   Platform 1 was recorded on 30th November 1985. This could accommodate 13 coaches, as could No. 2. The bay was numbered 3 and was for four coaches. Electric services through the station began on 5th December 1966. (D.A.Thompson)

67.   The 14.47 Crewe to Derby was worked by DMU no. 150107 on 7th April 1990. The bay platform is on the left; it had been used by trains for Market Drayton until 1956. (T.Heavyside)

68.   No. 390011 is on the left and no. 323238 is in the bay on 5th June 2010; the up through line had gone. Behind the camera is the signalling centre, which began life on 17th July 1966, but has evolved internally subsequently. (J.Whitehouse)

69.   Stoke North Junction is ¼ mile north of the station and branching from the down line is a single track to the Imerys china clay unloading depot. Nos 37087 and 37201 have arrived with a train, probably from Cornwall, in October 1995. (J.Whitehouse)

NEWCASTLE-UNDER-LYME

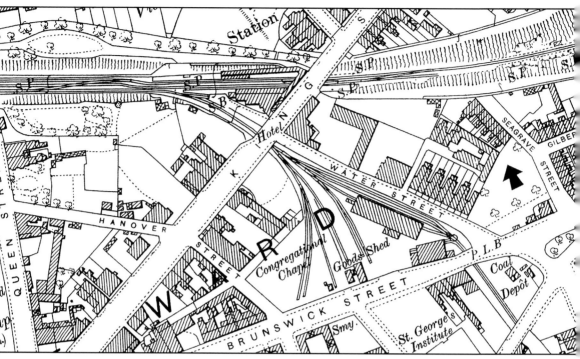

XVI. This 1900 extract has one siding passing under Brunswick Street from a wagon turntable, from which another runs into a secondary goods shed. The suffix was used from 1866, although it was "Lyne" until 1877. The population was high: 19,914 in 1901 and 76,910 in 1961.

70.   On the left are the windows of the signal box, which closed on 13th March 1966. Passenger service ceased on 2nd March 1964, when the trains were only running between Stoke-on-Trent and Silverdale. (P.Laming coll.)

71.　　One of the two ramps is visible; it links with the covered bridge to the booking office. On the right is the other side of the signal box. The locomotive is NSR class A 2-4-0T no. 35. (P.Laming coll.)

NEWCASTLE
(BRAMPTON) HALT

XVII.　This map overlaps the previous one, but does not show the halt, as it did not open until 1st May 1905. It was to the right of the footbridge and closed on 2nd April 1923, very early. Brampton Sidings Box had 23 levers and was open until 10th September 1967, when the route from the main line at Newcastle Junction closed.

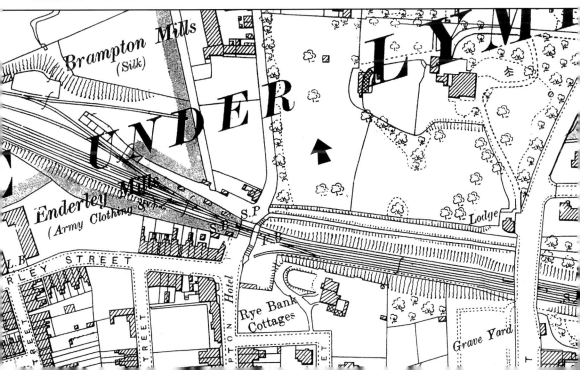

LIVERPOOL ROAD HALT

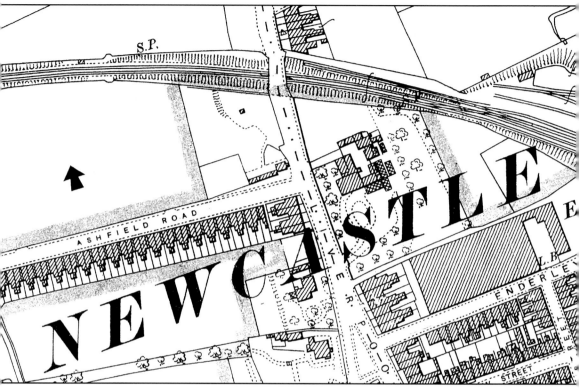

XVIII. A further extension of the same map omits the halt for the same reason. Again, it was to the east of the main road. The Potteries Electric Traction Company provided trams in the streets of the area from 15th May 1899 to 11th July 1928. They reached Newcastle on 17th March 1900.

72. The platforms were very short, as they were intended for railmotors. We look west from a passing train on 28th August 1954. Opened on 1st May 1905, closure was not until 2nd March 1964. (R.M.Casserley)

WEST OF NEWCASTLE

73.   Apedale Junction was ½ mile west of Liverpool Road Halt and the mineral line to Apedale Iron Works is shown between Knutton and Chesterton on map XIV. The northern part beyond Holditch Colliery was in use from 1853 to 1963 and the lower part lasted until 1991. From 1966 to that time, trains had to reverse here and run via Madeley. The nearby signal box had an 18-lever frame and closed on 24th September 1967. (M.Dart)

74.   Holditch Colliery was north of Knutton and its 1952 Sentinel no. 9543 was recorded on 11th July 1958. Sister no. 9534 can be found on the Foxfield Railway. The first shaft was sunk in 1912. A record extraction in one year of 400,000 tonnes was achieved in 1947, by about 1500 men. It was later noted for supplying record quantities of methane to local brickworks. (J.A.Peden/IRS)

75. Holditch Colliery was served by a short branch from Apedale Junction, which itself was the limit of working on the former Silverdale to Stoke-on-Trent line after that line closed as a through route in 1966. Holditch supplied coking coal to the British Steel Corporation as well as traffic to Rugeley 'A' power station. No. 47333 shunts vacuum-braked wagons on 5th January 1987. Rail traffic from Holditch ceased in 1989, but line closure was not until 1991. (P.D.Shannon)

76. This southward view from a railtour was taken on 22nd October 1989 and features Holditch Colliery. Knutton Halt had been west of Apedale Junction from 1st May 1905 until 20th September 1926. There had been a one mile long branch running south from Ketley's Sidings to a canal wharf. It had started from Silverdale in 1850 and was in use until 1864, although part of it, to Pool Dam, lasted until 1967. The halt dates were 1st May 1905 to 20th September 1926. (M.Dart)

SILVERDALE

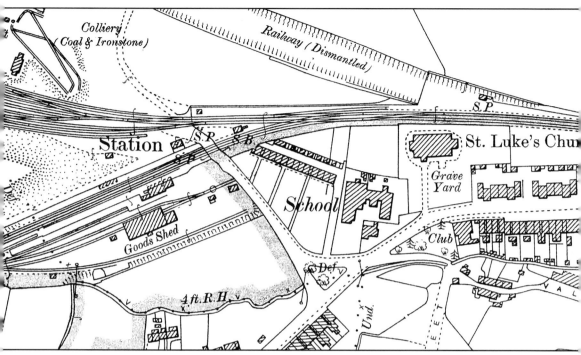

XIX.   Before reaching Silverdale, trains were able to call at Silverdale (Crown Street) Halt from 1st May 1905 until December 1945, although official closure was on 7th June 1949. This 1900 issue has the colliery lines top left and the route of the earlier tracks at the top. There were 7820 residents by 1901. The earthworks at the top had carried the original route to the Audley Branch.

77.   A postcard view east shows the spacious goods shed in about 1910. This station had opened with the extension to Market Drayton on 1st February 1870. The previous one was a terminus and had opened on 7th April 1862. It was a little to the east, north of St. Luke's Church. (P.Laming coll.)

78.   The date is 12th June 1948 and the train is the 4.50pm from Birmingham New Street. There were six private sidings nearby. There was a 7½ ton crane in the yard by 1938. (W.A.Camwell/SLS coll.)

79.   The down platform is seen on 28th August 1954. Many trains terminated at it and so the water supply at the far end would often be welcome. The NSR had been known widely as "The Knotty". (H.C.Casserley)

80.   The colliery lines can be glimpsed between the box and the arriving DMU. It would terminate here. Services to Market Drayton had ceased in 1956. The box had 40 levers and was built in 1934. It became a ground frame on 5th October 1964 and closed on 18th September 1971. The goods yard shut three weeks earlier. (W.A.Camwell/SLS coll.)

81.   We see the same train minutes later. Long after closure, the building was dismantled and rebuilt at the Apedale Heritage Centre (www.apedale.co.uk). In the distance is Silverdale Tunnel. DMUs were introduced on the service in 1956. (W.A.Camwell/SLS coll.)

82.	No. 47333 pauses at the former westbound platform at Silverdale with a loaded coal train from Holditch on 5th January 1987, while a merry-go-round train passes under the adjacent rapid loader. Silverdale station had closed to passengers on 2nd March 1964, but the building was still used by railway staff well into the 1980s. (P.D.Shannon)

83.	Silverdale pit had origins stretching back to 1830, but the National Coal Board completed a new mine on the site in 1950, which was to become the last surviving deep pit in Staffordshire, finally bowing out in December 1998. Its last operator was the independent firm Midland Mining, who took over from bankrupt Coal Investments in 1996. Merry-go-round trains ran from Silverdale to various power stations including Ironbridge and Fiddlers Ferry. No. 60047 runs round its empty train on 19th June 1993. (P.D.Shannon)

84.   No. 60047 draws forward with the 10.30 service to Fiddlers Ferry on 19th June 1993. It will reverse at Madeley Chord Junction and use the 1962 curve to gain access to the West Coast main line. Other destinations served from Silverdale in the 1990s were Rugeley and Didcot. The colliery operated until 1998, except for a break from 1993 to 1995. (P.D.Shannon)

85.   "The Cheshire Mole" railtour approaches the end of the branch on 7th November 1998, hauled by Load Haul's no. 60038. On the left is the shunters cabin. A bridge had to be built in 1961 to carry the line over the M6. On the other end of the same train was no. 56114 and they are approaching the old platforms. Peak outputs were over 750,000 tonnes per annum in the late 1970s, but new shafts in 1980 raised this to over a million. It was the last coal mine in The Potteries. (J.Whitehouse)

WEST OF SILVERDALE

86. This is the east portal of Silverdale Tunnel, which was 684yds long and is seen on 20th October 1989. Next was Keele Tunnel (321yds) and finally Stoney Low Tunnel (39yds). The latter two were south of Keele. There had been two single lines through this one, the one on the right being for Audley Branch trains. (M.Dart)

March 1951

Table 159 WELLINGTON, MARKET DRAYTON, CREWE, and MANCHESTER

Miles from Wellington		Week Days											Sundays			
		a.m	a.m	a.m		a.m		W	Z	p.m	p.m		a.m		p.m	
	153 London (Pad.).... dep	12n5	..	7 5	..	9 10	..	11 10	11 10	2 10	5N10	..	12A5	..	6 10	..
	153 Birmingham (S.H.) "	6 0	8 22	1035	..	11 55	..	1 42	1 42	4 41	7N40	..	7 0	..	8 58	..
	164 Worcester (S.H.) 153	..	6 33	9 35	..	..	..	10T58	10T58	..	6 30	..	..	..	4T16	..
	153 Shrewsbury ...... "	6 35	8 37	1123	..	12 20	..	2 25	2 25	5 10	8 10	..	8 0	..	9 12	..
—	Wellington......... dep	7 30	10 0	1215	..	1 0	..	2 45	2 45	5 55	9 25	..	9 15	..	1055	..
2¼	Longdon Halt..........	..	10 4	1219	..	1 4	..	2 49	2 49	5 59	Zz	..	9 20	..	Zz	..
4½	Crudgington...........	7 37	10 9	1225	..	1 9	..	2 54	2 54	6 5	9 35	..	9 25	..	11 7	..
7	Rowton Halt...........	..	1013	1229	..	1 13	..	2 58	2 58	6 9	9F39	..	9 29	..	..	..
7½	Ellerdine Halt..........	7 43	1017	1233	..	1 17	..	3 1	3 1	6 13	9 43	..	9 33	..	..	..
8¾	Peplow	7 47	1022	1238	..	1 21	..	3 6	3 6	6 17	9 48	..	9 37	..	1117	..
11	Hodnet................	7 53	1027	1243	..	1 26	..	3 11	3 11	6 22	9 53	..	9 42	..	1124	..
12	Wollerton Halt..........	7 57	1030	1246	..	1 29	..	3 14	3 14	6 25	..	..	9 45	..	..	..
13¾	Tern Hill..............	8 2	1035	1251	..	1 35	..	3 19	3 19	6 30	9 58	..	9 50	..	1133	..
16¾	Market Drayton arr	8 9	1042	1257	..	1 42	..	3 26	3 26	6 37	10 5	..	9 56	..	1140	..
	Market Drayton dep	8 12	1045	1 2	..	..	..	3 28	..	6 41	10 9	..	10 0	..	1144	..
20½	Adderley	8 20	1050	1 8	..	..	..	3 34	..	6 47	1016	..	10 5	..	1152	..
21½	Coxbank Halt...........	8 23	1053	1 11	..	..	..	3 37	..	6 51	1020	..	10 8	..	..	..
22	Audlem................	8 26	1057	1 15	..	..	..	3 40	..	6 55	1023	..	1011	..	1159	..
24½	Coole Pilate Halt........	8 32	11 2	1 20	..	..	..	3 45	..	7 0	..	..	1016	..	..	..
27½	Nantwich..............	8 38	11 9	1 27	..	..	..	3 51	..	7 8	1033	..	1022	..	1217	..
29½	Willaston	..	..	..	..	..	..	..	..	..	..	..	..	..	..	..
32	Crewe............ arr	8 49	1121	1 38	..	..	..	4 0	..	7 18	1042	..	1033	..	1230	..
62¾	523 Manchester (L.R.) arr	9K49	1255	2 35	..	..	..	5 20	..	8 45	1a32	..	1136	..	1V32	..

Mls frm Crewe		Week Days											Sundays			
		a.m	a.m		a.m	a.m		p.m	W	p.m	p.m		a.m		p.m	
	524 Manchester (L.R.) dep	12 30	..	..	8 5	11 10	..	Z	1 18	3U20	7 10	..	11A55	..	7 5	..
	Crewe............ dep	6 5	..	..	9 30	12 52	..	..	3 15	5 10	8 50	..	6 40	..	8 35	..
2¾	Willaston	..	..	..	..	..	..	..	..	5 15	..	..	..	..	..	..
4½	Nantwich..............	6 13	..	..	9 38	1 2	..	..	3 23	5 20	8 58	..	6 48	..	8 43	..
7½	Coole Pilate Halt.......	..	..	..	9 45	1 9	..	..	3 29	5 27	9 4	..	6 55	..	..	..
10	Audlem................	6 23	..	..	9 48	1 13	..	..	3 33	5 31	9 9	..	7 0	..	8 52	..
10½	Coxbank Halt...........	6 26	..	..	9 51	1 17	..	..	3 36	5 34	9 12	..	7 5	..	Aa	..
11½	Adderley	6 30	..	..	9 54	1 20	..	..	3 39	5 37	9 16	..	7 8	..	8 57	..
15½	Market Drayton arr	6 37	..	..	10 1	1 27	..	..	3 46	5 44	9 23	..	7 14	..	9 3	..
	Market Drayton dep	6 41	8 0	..	10 3	1 29	..	3 50	3 50	5 49	9 25	..	7 20	..	9 5	..
18½	Tern Hill..............	6 48	8 6	..	10 9	1 35	..	3 55	3 55	5 55	9 32	..	7 25	..	9 10	..
20	Wollerton Halt	..	8 10	..	10 13	1 39	..	3 59	3 59	5 59	..	..	7 28	..	..	..
21	Hodnet................	6 57	8 14	..	10 16	1 43	..	4 2	4 2	6 2	9 39	..	7 32	..	9 15	..
23¼	Peplow	7 3	8 19	..	10 21	1 48	..	4 7	4 7	6 7	9 44	..	7 37	..	9 20	..
24½	Ellerdine Halt..........	..	8 23	..	10 25	1 52	..	4 11	4 11	6 11	..	..	7 40	..	..	..
25	Rowton Halt............	7P10	8 27	..	10 28	1 55	..	4 14	4 14	6F15	..	..	7 45	..	..	..
27½	Crudgington............	7 15	8 32	..	10 32	2 0	..	4 18	4 18	6 19	9 53	..	7 50	..	9 30	..
29¾	Longdon Halt...........	7 20	8 38	..	10 37	2 5	..	4 23	4 23	6S24	..	..	7 54	..	..	..
32	Wellington......... arr	7 28	8 45	..	10 43	2 13	..	4 35	4 35	6 31	10 4	..	8 1	..	9 39	..
42½	153 Shrewsbury .... arr	8 32	9 40	..	11 48	2 51	..	5 24	5 24	7 34	1028	..	8 59	..	1050	..
85	164 Worcester (S.H) 153	..	12 5	..	1 55	5 41	..	8 28	8 28	9 55	..	..	12Z55	..	..	..
64	153 Birmingham (S.H.) "	8 55	9 55	..	11 55	3 50	..	5 53	5 53	7 45	1210	..	9 49	..	..	..
174½	153 London (Padd'ton) "	11 20	12 25	..	2 35	7§45	..	8 40	8 40	11 25	5 5	..	2 20	..	..	..

A Saturday nights
Aa Calls to set down only on notice being given to the Guard at Audlem
a a.m.
F Thurdays and Saturdays
K Arr. 10 31 a.m. on Saturdays
N Dep. London (Pad.) 410 and Birmingham (Snow Hill) 7 18 p.m. on Saturdays.
n Night
P Calls to take up only on giving the necessary hand signal to the Driver
S Saturdays only.
T Foregate St.
U Mayfield Station.
V Monday morn.
W Wednesdays and Saturdays
Z Except Wednesdays and Saturdays
Z Foregate Street. Arr. 11T40 a.m. commencing 6th May
Zz Calls to set down only.
§ Arr. 7 5 p.m. on Mondays

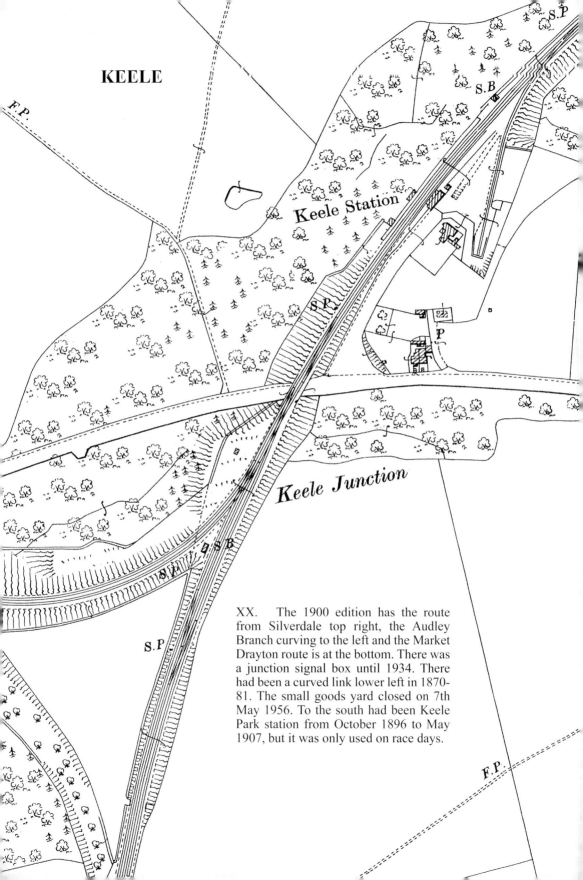

KEELE

F.P.

S.P.

S.B.

Keele Station

S.P.

P

Keele Junction

S.P.

S.P.

F.P.

XX.   The 1900 edition has the route from Silverdale top right, the Audley Branch curving to the left and the Market Drayton route is at the bottom. There was a junction signal box until 1934. There had been a curved link lower left in 1870-81. The small goods yard closed on 7th May 1956. To the south had been Keele Park station from October 1896 to May 1907, but it was only used on race days.

87.   This is a northward view on 30th April 1933. The line to the goods yard curves to the right, beyond the snow. (Bentley coll.)

88.   Here we look south in 1958, two years after the last passenger had used the platform on the left. The right one closed in 1931. There were 1114 residents in 1901, 1529 in 1961, a university was established in 1962 and a medical school followed in 2007. (Stations UK)

4. Audley Branch
LEYCETT

89.   The first three stations on the branch were opened on 26th June 1880; all four were photographed in about 1890 and closed on 27th April 1931. The northern and southern ones were of similar design. (A.Dudman coll.)

HALMEREND

90.   The station was a basic all timber construction. Several trains from the south terminated here for many years. (A. Dudman coll.)

AUDLEY AND BIGNALL END

91.   Diglake Colliery is on the right. The suffix "Bignall End" was added on 9th July 1923. "Audley End" is in Essex and so confusion could continue in some minds. (A. Dudman coll.)

ALSAGER ROAD

92.   This station opened on 1st July 1889, but did not have platforms on the Crewe-Harecastle route, which is in the background. The name was TALK & ALSAGER ROAD until 1st November 1902. Many trains on the route ran between Harecastle and Stoke. (A.Dudman coll.)

5. From Madeley Road

NORTH OF MADELEY ROAD

93.   The route from Stoke passes over the Stafford-Crewe main line, but in 1962 a single line connection was made between the two. This was to enable coal from Silverdale to reach Crewe for distribution. The single line from the former is in the distance and is seen from a railtour on the loop. (M.Dart)

94.   No. 60045 *Josephine Butler* is running onto the loop in December 1992, having brought empty stock from one of the extensive yards south of Crewe. It will soon run round its train on the loop and go off to the right, over the main line. Madeley station was on that route until closure in 1952. It can be found in pictures 37 and 38 in our *Stafford to Chester* album. Madeley Chord was not used after December 1998. (J.Whitehouse)

MADELEY ROAD

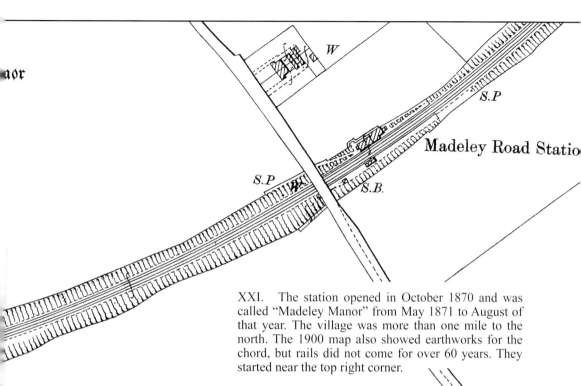

ıɒɾ

W

S.P

Madeley Road Statio

S.P

S.B.

XXI.   The station opened in October 1870 and was called "Madeley Manor" from May 1871 to August of that year. The village was more than one mile to the north. The 1900 map also showed earthworks for the chord, but rails did not come for over 60 years. They started near the top right corner.

95.   An eastward panorama in 1949 shows the platforms which were last used on 20th July 1931. The line was a through route for freight until 1966, notably coal to power stations. The building had been used as a dwelling until demolished in 1979. (Stations UK)

PIPE GATE

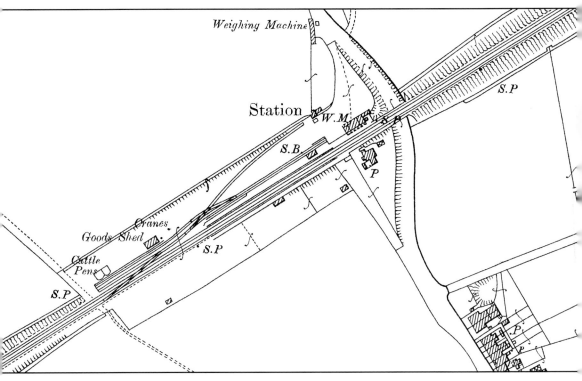

XXII   This 1902 extract shows the station as being close to the village and that there were two cranes and also two weighing machines.

96.   An Edwardian postcard shows the staff crossing boards extended over the rodding tunnel to the NSR signal box, which was in use until route closure on 8th March 1966. (LOSA)

97.   No. 42119 is northbound in about 1950, when a telegram service was still on offer to the public and one small oil lamp was deemed sufficient for lighting the area. Average passenger numbers in 1956 on the first train were 9, the second one 12 and the third 3.
(N.R.Knight/SLS coll.)

98.   We look towards Market Drayton on 28th August 1954. Local passengers were served until 7th May 1956, but racegoers came and went until 1963. (R.M.Casserley)

99.   The additional building does not appear in picture 96. Being heated, it was probably the goods office. This and the next picture are from June 1967. The line from Silverdale had been singled in 1934. (R.J.Essery/R.S.Carpenter coll.)

100.   This is the station approach, the main road passing under the line to the left. Local goods traffic had continued until 1st February 1963. A very important traffic item had been milk for a long time. A large creamery was built south of the station in 1935, complete with sidings, but the 1955 rail strike damaged the traffic. (R.J.Essery/R.S.Carpenter coll.)

NORTON-IN-HALES

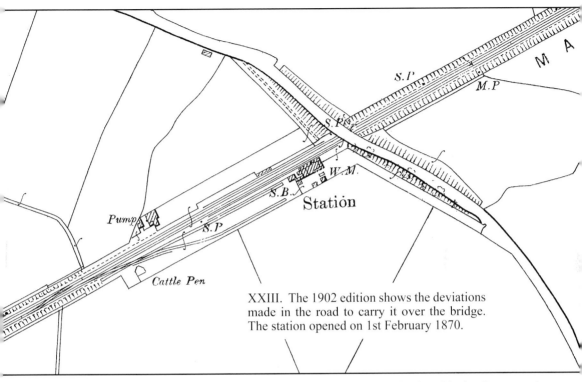

XXIII. The 1902 edition shows the deviations made in the road to carry it over the bridge. The station opened on 1st February 1870.

101.   We glimpse at the down platform on 28th August 1954, along with the white loading gauge in the distance. Passengers vanished on 7th May 1956, as did local freight traffic. (R.M.Casserley)

102.   The remaining single track was photographed on 17th June 1967. This was the first station on the route in Shropshire. The building later became a dwelling. (R.J.Essery/R.S.Carpenter coll.)

103.   The end of the NSR from Stoke was at Silverdale Junction. The box was built by the GWR in 1893; its 48-lever frame ceased to be used on 16th May 1967. It is seen a month later, with the Silverdale lines on the right and their speed limit sign on the left. (R.J.Essery/R.S.Carpenter coll.)

6. Market Drayton

XXIV. The main map is from 1902 and north of the 40ft turntable is the single road NSR engine shed, which closed in April 1931. Inset is the location map, which is at 4 miles to 1 inch and is from 1946. The ex-NSR route is branching right and was singled in May 1935.

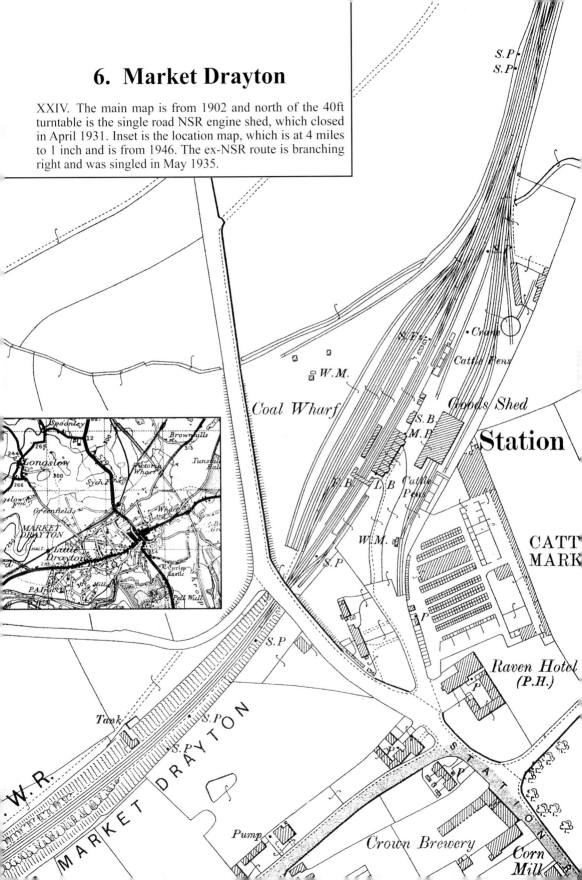

S.P.
S.P.

Crane

W.M.

Cattle Pens

Coal Wharf

Goods Shed

S.B.
M.P.

Station

F.B. T.B. Cattle Pens

W.M.

S.P.

CATT
MARK

S.P.

Raven Hotel
(P.H.)

Tank

S.P.

S.P

W.R.

M A R K E T   D R A Y T O N

S T A T I O N

Pump

Crown Brewery

Corn
Milk

Inset (location map)

Spoonley

Brownhills

Longslow

Tunstall
Hall

Sych Field

Greenfield

Wharf

MARKET
DRAYTON

Little
Drayton

104.   A northward panorama from the road bridge shows a horse in the station approach and the roof of the cattle market beyond. The railway cattle pens were adjacent to it. The GWR staff numbered 15 in 1870, 30 in 1903 and 25 in 1933. The NSR had 17 men in 1870. (P.Laming coll.)

105.   A closer postcard view has the 1870 platform face on the left, which was added for NSR trains. There were buffer stops at the south end of the line until 1877. (Stations UK)

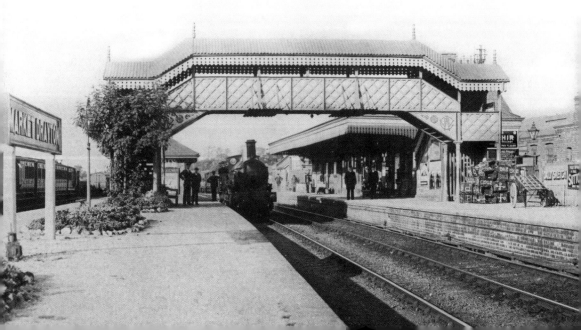

106.   The engine shed was photographed shortly before its closure in 1931. Water was pumped by steam from a well. The first turntable was 35ft long; a 40ft one arrived in 1880. An 0-6-0 and an 0-6-0T were the normal residents. (R.M.Casserley coll.)

107.   We are at the south end of the station on 30th April 1933 and running round its train is LMS no. 2347. The ground signal is set for the crossover to be used. (H.C.Casserley)

2nd- HALF DAY EXCURSION	HALF DAY EXCURSION -2nd
8th August, 1963	8th August, 1963
Market Drayton to SILVERDALE (Staffs)	Silverdale (Staffs) to MARKET DRAYTON
(M) Fare 2/6	Fare 2/6 (M)
For conditions see over	For conditions see over

0079   0079

N.S.R.—THIRD CLASS.
SILVERDALE To
NEWCASTLE-U-L
Available for one journey on day of issue only
W
Turn over   Newcas   170   Fare 3d.

6103

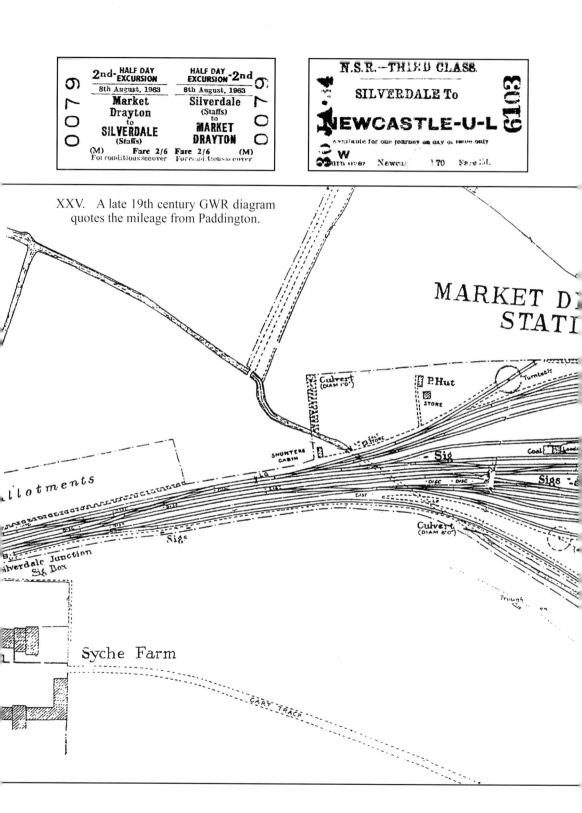

XXV. A late 19th century GWR diagram
quotes the mileage from Paddington.

MARKET D
STATI

Culvert (DIAM 1'0")

P.Hut
STORE
Turntable

Coal

Sig

Sigs

SHUNTERS CABIN

Sig

DISC   DISC

Allotments

Culvert (DIAM 6'0")

Sigs

Silverdale Junction
Sig Box

Trough

Syche Farm

CART TRACK

ORDER FORM

- Albums contain 96 **pages** and at least 120 photographs, together with large scale maps
details of local history interest. All publications are bound in attractive glossy hard covers, unless
stated.

- **ALBUMS** hardback - unless otherwise stated £18.95 see below for postage
- Pre-Order RAIL TIMES FOR GREAT BRITAIN £26.00 plus £5.75 P&P (UK)

GE - Personal orders - 2nd class   POST FREE
     1st class   £1.50 per book
     Overseas   At cost

Trade orders - UK (5 books or more)   POST FREE   FREE
    UK (4 books or less)   £1.35 per book
Overseas - Europe, Surface Mail and Air Mail elsewhere   See website for postal charges

ENT - Please enclose a cheque with your order made payable to Middleton Press or complete the details
you wish to pay by credit/debit card, alternatively you can order on line www.middletonpress.co.uk

Postal Order ___ or Card details below ___

ard __

xpiry date ____ / ____   3 digit security number ___ ___ ___

(as it shows on the card)

RESS

POST CODE

NE NUMBER (daytime)

RDER -

ISBN:
ISBN:
ISBN:
ISBN:
ISBN:

ONE NUMBER (daytime)   Order value: £

stomer Signature

Middleton Press

Easebourne Lane, Midhurst, West Sussex. GU29 9AZ
Tel: 01730 813169 Fax: 01730 812601
Email: info@middletonpress.co.uk www.middletonpress.co.uk

NEW -

Reprints -

BRANCH LINES AROUND WISBECH

PEEBLES LOOP

BRANCH LINES TO SEATON & SIDMOUTH

KINGS LYNN TO HUNSTANTON

HEXHAM TO HAWICK

SOUTH LYNN TO NORWICH CITY

YEOVIL TO EXETER

BATH TO EVERCREECH JUNCTION

BATH GREEN PARK TO BRISTOL

BURNHAM TO EVERCREECH JUNCTION

BRANCH LINE TO ILFRACOMBE

DERBY TO CHESTERFIELD

ST ALBANS TO BEDFORD

WOKING TO PORTSMOUTH

ST PANCRAS TO ST ALBANS

Albums £18.95 free P&P (UK)

GREAT RAILWAY ARMCHAIR JOURNEYS

RAILWAY LEAFLET
FULL BROCHURE UPON REQUEST

EVOLVING THE ULTIMATE RAIL ENCYCLOPEDIA INTERNATIONAL

SEPTEMBER - NOVEMBER 2019

..... follow our latest news on twitter & facebook -

NEW   Published 21 September

UTTOXETOR TO BUXTON
VIA ASHBOURNE Vic Mitchell and Keith Smith
The line will interest most people as it closed early and ran through superb scenery. It began in the Dove Valley and ran through the south of the Peak District. The trains varied greatly and many carried much limestone. Walkers can now use the Tissington Trail to enjoy much of the route herein.

NEW   Published 19 October

CROMFORD AND HIGH PEAK
BY RAIL and TRAIL Vic Mitchell and Keith Smith
This unusual route began as a link between canals east and west of the Pennine Peaks, which were too high for boats. It only ever carried goods regularly, due to the steep gradients and cable-worked inclines. Herein are answers to the trail walker's many questions.

NEW   Published 23 November

NEWCASTLE TO ALNMOUTH
AND THE AMBLE BRANCH
Roger R Darsley and Dennis A Lovett
This journey on one of the country's premier routes, leaves Newcastle Central and travels through the city's northern suburbs, then the collieries of the South East coalfield to end at Alnmouth in the history and beauty of Northumberland.

NEW   Available for Pre-Order

RAIL TIMES FOR GREAT BRITAIN
The complete set of public timetables from Network Rail are presented in one volume in their recent style. Their earlier style of National Route diagrams have been retained and updated by us. *A separate folded wall version is also available.*
(release date depends on NR) valid from 14 Dec - 17 May 2020

Reprints ....

**BRANCH LINES AROUND WISBECH * PEEBLES LOOP
BRANCH LINES TO SEATON & SIDMOUTH * KINGS LYNN TO HUNSTANTON
HEXHAM TO HAWICK * SOUTH LYNN TO NORWICH CITY * YEOVIL TO EXETER
BATH TO EVERCREECH JUNCTION * BATH GREEN PARK TO BRISTOL
BURNHAM TO EVERCREECH JUNCTION * BRANCH LINE TO ILFRACOMBE
DERBY TO CHESTERFIELD * ST ALBANS TO BEDFORD
WOKING TO PORTSMOUTH * DOUGLAS TO RAMSEY * ST PANCRAS TO ST ALBANS**

Middleton Press Ltd.

Each album takes you on a journey between the towns listed or to the branch terminus.

At each station, the pictures are in date order to give you a historical tour.

INDEX TO STATIONS

in **MP** albums

visit our website and view QUICK DOWNLOADS".

Or just telephone us with the name of your favourite station and the correct album will soon be revealed.

www. middletonpress. co.uk

MP Middleton Press
EVOLVING THE ULTIMATE RAIL ENCYCLOPEDIA

— ISBN PREFIXES —
A - 978 0 906520
B - 978 1 873793   C - 978 1 901706   D - 978 1 904474
E - 978 1 906008   F - 978 1 908174   G - 978 1 910356

Here is our list of **RAILWAY** titles. Please check current availability by looking at www.middletonpress.co.uk or by telephoning us. Also available are our **Bradshaws, Tramways, Trolleybus, Military** and **Coastal** series. Please request a full brochure for further details.

See **www.middletonpress.co.uk** for details
of **Comprehensive RAIL TIMES** for Great Britain

to use the **INDEX TO STATIONS** visit
our website and view **"QUICK DOWNLOADS"**

RAIL TIMES FOR GREAT BRITAIN please request details

ALBUM
and othe
otherwis

PRICE

POST

PAYM
below

Chequ
Visa
Mast

Card

NAM

ADD

PH

3rd-SINGLE   SINGLE-3rd
Pipe Gate to
Pipe Gate   Pipe Gate
Market Drayton   Keele
KEELE or
MARKET DRAYTON
3296   3296
(M) 0/11 FARE 0/11 (M)
For conditions see over   For conditions see over

N.S.R. PARLIAMENTARY.
NORTON-IN-HALES To
MARKET DRAYTON
AVAILABLE FOR ONE JOURNEY ON DAY OF ISSUE ONLY
4245
Turn over   Mkt. Drayton 60   Fare 3d.

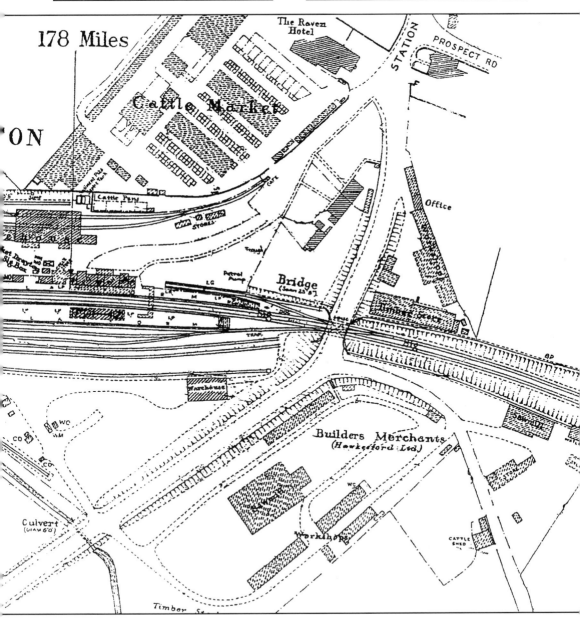

178 Miles

108.   Waiting to depart minutes later is the 10.21am to Stoke, hauled by 2-6-4T class 4P no. 2347. All the buildings date from the period of alterations in 1880-1900. (H.C.Casserley)

109.   Another shot on the same day features GWR "Barnum" class 2-4-0 no. 3223 leaving with the 9.40am from Wellington. (H.C.Casserley)

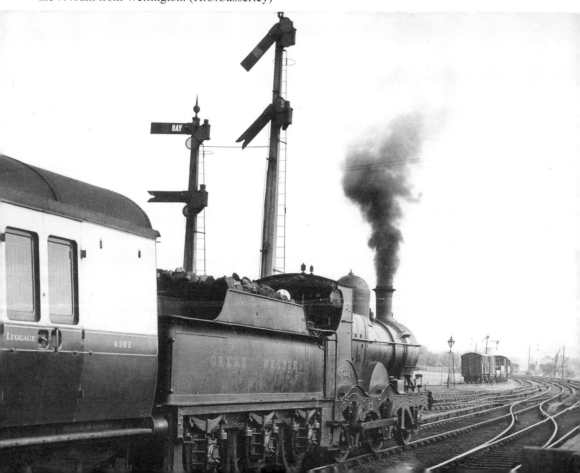

110.   Working the 8.42am train to Crewe on 28th August 1954 is no. 42235, an ex-LMS class 4 2-6-4T. A mobile crane is included; the one in the goods yard was rated at 6 tons. (H.C.Casserley)

111.   An SLS special train is about to depart north in early 1958, a time when trespass rules were not enforced. "The Pines Express" passed this way between Manchester and the South Coast between 1910 and 1967, except in some war years. (Stations UK)

112.   Another SLS tour train and 2-6-4T no. 42482 waits to depart for Stoke on 31st May 1958. This was an ex-LMS class 4, a successful type introduced in 1927. The route had not carried passengers for two years. (G.Adams/A.Carlton coll)

113.   It is 10th May 1959 and we can enjoy the uninterrupted panorama northwards. The signals for Silverdale Junction are in the distance. (P.J.Garland/R.S.Carpenter coll)

114.   Recorded on the same day are the delightful details of the footbridge, notably the handrail castings. A Sugg's Rochester pattern gas lamp is included. This design was free of shadows. (P.J.Garland/R.S.Carpenter coll)

115.   Livestock wagon movements numbered 249 in 1913, but only 17 by 1931. Much of the massive goods shed is visible in this view south on the same occasion. (P.J.Garland/R.S.Carpenter coll.)

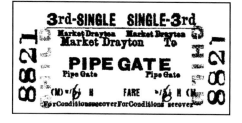

3rd-SINGLE SINGLE-3rd
Market Drayton Market Drayton
Market Drayton   To
PIPE GATE
Pipe Gate   Pipe Gate
(MO   6   N   FARE   N (M
For Conditions see cover For Conditions see cover

8821   8821

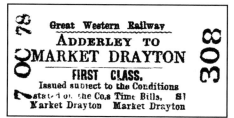

Great Western Railway
ADDERLEY TO
MARKET DRAYTON
FIRST CLASS.
Issued subject to the Conditions
stated on the Co.s Time Bills,   SI
Market Drayton   Market Drayton

70078   308

116.   It is 2nd August 1959 and the flower beds are still well tended and all but one coal wagon are of steel construction. Coal received in 1923 weighed 555 tons, but other minerals amounted to 30,738 tons, probably due to road surfacing. (G.Adams/M.J.Stretton coll.)

117.   Normal platform ramps were replaced by smaller angled ones. The number of parcels changing trains here would have been tremendous. Working the 8.42pm to Stoke on 27th August 1959 is no. 42235, another class 4 2-6-4T. (R.M.Casserley)

118.   Station Box was completed in 1893 and had 47 levers. It closed on 6th March 1967, as did the goods yard here and all the routes. The view is from 29th July 1961 and shows 0-6-0PT no. 9774 with the 12.50pm from Wellington. (E.Wilmshurst)

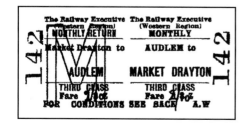

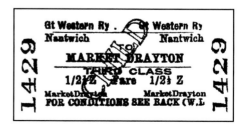

119.   Ex-GWR 0-6-0PT no. 3744 was working to Nantwich sometime in 1962. The ventilation for the gents is discreet, but the WAY OUT is just the reverse. The site is now occupied by factories. (A.W.V.Mace/Milepost 92½)

120.   As we leave the station on 1st July 1962, we see the WAY IN, albeit in shadow. This style of GWR station can still be enjoyed, with steam trains in attendance, at Kidderminster, on the Severn Valley Railway. (Bentley coll.)

MP **Middleton Press**

EVOLVING THE ULTIMATE RAIL ENCYCLOPEDIA

Easebourne Lane, Midhurst, West Sussex.
GU29 9AZ   Tel:01730 813169

www.middletonpress.co.uk   email:info@middletonpress.co.uk
A-978 0 906520 B- 978 1 873793 C- 978 1 901706 D-978 1 904474
E - 978 1 906008 F - 978 1 908174

All titles listed below were in print at time of publication - please check current availability by looking at our
website - *www.middletonpress.co.uk* or by requesting a Brochure which includes our
LATEST RAILWAY TITLES also our TRAMWAY, TROLLEYBUS, MILITARY and COASTAL series